FEEL THE CHANGE

NITESH MORE

Contents

Contents

" If you don't do anything today, Don't expect, Tomorrow will be different. - Nitesh More. "

Feel The Change

Feel The Change

If you are looking for a change in your life then you must feel the change before change is going to happen. You must inform to your brain that I want to change. Once you inform, Our brain started to take an action on that because It has a tremendous power to bring that change in our life.

Nowadays, Everyone is struggling and we really need a changes in our life but before having a change, You must ask to yourself...

Why I want to change ?

Why I need a changes in my life ?

For whom, I am changing ?

Have I forgotten to live a life ?

Why so much of frustration ?

Why anger is coming on small things ?

Am I lost ?

Whatever happened, It is happened but by thinking of that, You can't change. Either you should feel the change or fear the change. Better you should feel the change because It is you, Who have got this beautiful life. Isn't it ?

Why focus ?

Where to focus ?

Whom to focus ?

Nothing is changed and nothing will be changed until you focus on your goal to have a better tomorrow.

Everyone is busy for something for somewhere and the saddest part is that He or she even does not know that, Why are they so busy ? Are they really busy ? or just a show off....? They are busy in unwanted stuff and They also know very well but still, They love to do that because their focus is on something else.

I am dedicating this book to all those peoples who were, is and will be with me in my good and bad times.

THANK YOU VERY VERY MUCH.

" I am the product of my life and I make sure that I be the best of the best product of my life. - Nitesh More. "

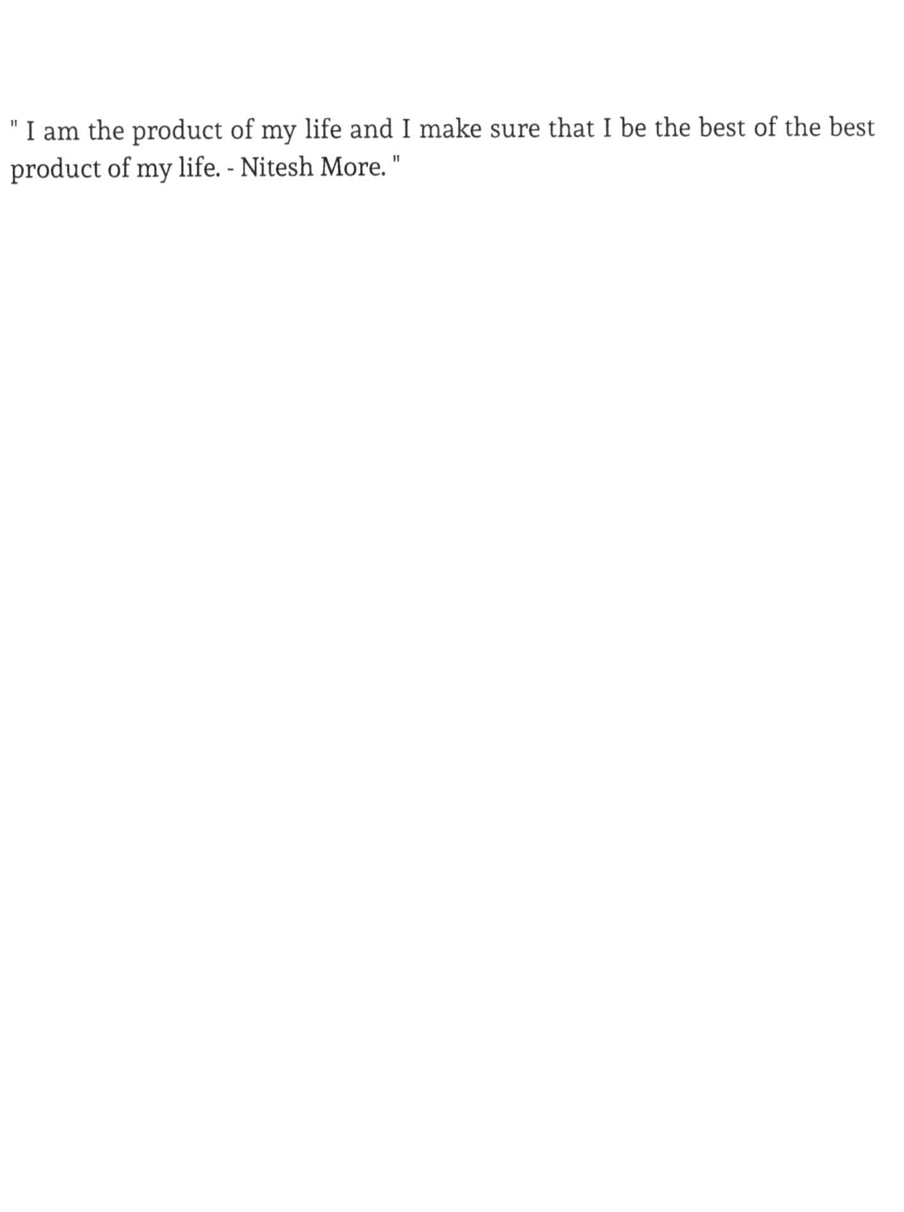

I

ALONE

BY LIVING ALONE,

IF YOU GET THE HAPPINESS, KEEP ON LIVING.

WHO CARES..?

IF YOU DON'T CARE ABOUT YOURSELF, THEN WHO WILL...?

It is all happened because of you. You are like this and you can't improve. We are and we will also be with you in the problem....therefore, there is no need to come here from today.

After reading,

What do you feel ?

ALONE,

It looks like someone has a loan and whose loan is due, how can he/she will spend a time together ?

Alone word is a very small but It is very dangerous for them, who is going by tough time.

If I ask..?

Being alone is right or wrong?

May be,

It is good for them, who wants to live an alone life.

May be,

It is very dangerous for them, Who became an alone because of some reasons.

Similar like every coin has two sides.

People living alone neither talk to anyone nor they open up quickly with anyone.

Perhaps they don't like to talk to anybody.

Those peoples always find a space to hide from people. The problem is not that, those people are alone but the problem is that they have decided in their mind that, They are alone in this world.

My life is like this and I will live a life like this throughout of my life.

According to me,

Those people do not take any interest in anything.

Those people hate life.

Those people get angry soon.

Perhaps, they feel that this is the routine of our life and It will be like this...

But the truth is something else,

Alone people must know that life will not change until you change.

I would like to say that,

You too can have a better life.

We have a family.

We have a friends.

We have a guests.

We have a special person...with whom you love to spend your entire life.

And so many other relations....

Right.

Then why are you feeling alone ?

Connect with each other and see the magic.

Change will come,

If you want to change your life, otherwise yesterday, today, tomorrow will be the same as it is.

Have you forgotten the good moments?

How can you forget this?

When you are alone,

Just remember your old memories, you will feel good. Most of the time, when we feel alone, we start hating others and even god too...

Sometimes, we ask to god that Why did this happen to me ?

Why I am alone in this world.

Who took my smile ?

Everyday is a new day and Everyday, we get an opportunity to have a positive life.

Always think positive, If he or she can have a better life then, Definitely I can also have a better life.

I can also have a positive life.

We have a one life and in that also, you are living an alone life.
How sad it is ?

- I am not alone. There are so many relations.

- I can be a change of my life.

- I can enjoy my life.

- I am in this world to have a better life.

Quote No - 1

" Be busy to be lazy. Choice is yours but please choose carefully, because this is your life, No one else. - Nitesh More. "

II
MONEY

MONEY IS IMPORTANT IN OUR LIFE.

DO YOU REALLY EARN A MONEY IN A RIGHT WAY....BECAUSE MONEY HAS KILLED OUR OWN HAPPINESS, NOT OWN BUT FAMILY HAPPINESS TOO.

Does money really make us happy ?

Whatever your answer, I can only say that happiness can not be bought with money.

Today, peoples are very sad because they are running after money and the worst thing is that, they are ready to do anything in a wrong way to get the money.

Just imagine,

If the same person runs towards his goal then I guarantee you, Money will run after him.

We have forgotten that we have made the money and not the money made us. We have seen in the news that today, there is a fight in the family for the money. Today, there is an enmity between friends because of money. Today, there is relationship broken because of money and so on...but the main question is, Do we really get happiness by money ?

I am sorry to say but we have really forgotten.

Money can only meet our needs.

Whatever your need is..,in your hand only.

Can you imagine about artist ?

An artist is the person who put everything to fit in the character.

How many hours of shooting ?

How many months on diet ?

How many sacrifices they do ?

Is that only for the money ?

Or just to improve themselves to live a life of a character and you know this very well.

We have only one life and in that too, Most of the time, we are running behind the money. If the bank balance increases,

Will that give you a peace ?

Is it possible ?

Let me tell you a story,

There were a two friends.

One is a Gopi and other one is a Topi.

They used to spend a most of the time together but topi was sad because

He had no money and gopi was happy because he does not take any tension about money.

One day,

They went to the temple and started asking something from a god.

The Topi asked to gopi, what do you want from a god ?

He said, Nothing except to keep everyone happy in this world.

After hearing this,

Topi started laughing and saying that you are a crazy. You had got the opportunity to ask anything but you asked nothing. You are a really crazy.

Then gopi asked to topi, what do you want from god ?

Topi said, just the money should come and this sequence should not stop.

Gopi is just looking at him. He did not say anything.

They are going from there.

After few years,

They met but no one had expected that something will be happened like this.......

Topi, who was making a money by sitting outside the temple as a beggar and who was thinking about others.., gopi was worshiping in the temple with the entire family.

Moral is that, don't let money dominate your life because we can buy a things from a money, not happiness.

Focus on a goal, not on a money.

Focus on a good things, good things will happen.

- Do not run for a money. Let's money run behind you.

- Invest yourself, money will come automatically.

• 9 •

- Earn in a right way with respect.

- You have an abilities to earn a money. Discover yourself.

Quote No - 2

" The day, When you start loving your work..., From that day, Work will start loving you. - Nitesh More. "

III

YOU ARE WHAT YOU THINK

YOU ARE THE PRODUCT OF YOUR THINKING. IF YOU WANT TO BE A BETTER PRODUCT OF YOUR LIFE.

THINK BETTER AND BE BETTER.

It does not matter,

What people think about yourself, but what you think about yourself makes a lot of differences.

It does not matter,

How do you look ?

What do you wear ?

What product do you use ?

What brand of shoes, do you wear ?

How many people know you ?

What type of job, do you do ?

What type of business, do you do ?

Which newspaper, do you read ?

How big is your house ?

In which area, do you love ?

Do you love yourself or not ?

It does not matter to anyone but this matter makes a difference to you or does not...that is most important than anything else.

If you want the right answer, then stand in front of the mirror,

You will know, who is your competitor ?
Your fight is with yourself, and not with anyone else.
Outside fighting always hurts itself and it's bruised family suffers.
Fighting with yourself always helps to make a better.
You know,
You should think big and good because what you think, you become.
May be,
You fell down in life.
May be,
You are a failure.
May be,
Your time is bad.
But even then, do not drop your thinking because that's the only one thing that helps you to make a success with failure and finally, Whatever, However, you think about yourself that helps you to become a what you think.

- You are today because of your thinking.

- You can be what you want to be.

- Always be in a present.

- Do what you love.

Quote No - 3

" When you focus on a problem, You create more problems but when you focus on a solutions..., You create more opportunities. - Nitesh More. "

IV

GOOD THINKING

GOOD THINKING CAN MAKE YOUR LIFE EASY AND SIMPLE.

ARE YOU A GOOD THINKER ?

Good thinking can change your entire life. Similarly, Bad thinking can destroy your entire life.

Thinking is all about brain.

Do you really use your brain ?

Which thinking, do you want to keep ?

Obviously, Good thinking.

Let's talk about good thinking.

Good thinking people always talk about solutions. They don't have any problem with problems because they see problem as an opportunity.

Good thinking people always welcome the problems on their side so that they can learn something from those problems to get a better experience to make themselves strong.

Good thinking people do not see who is right or who is wrong, but they see only what can be a right.

Good thinking people always ask themselves, what is inside me that is stopping me to have a better life.

Good thinking people does not allow negative words, negative vibes in their life.

Good thinking people always keep themselves positive and together they spread a positivity.

Good thinking people always ready to learn something new because knowledge helps to succeed.

Good thinking people always believe in....I can do anyhow.

- **To have a good thoughts.**

- **To make a difference by your thinking.**

- **To be positive in any situation.**

- **To be happy.**

Quote No - 4

" Nobody can make you sad until you give them a permission to make you sad. - Nitesh more. "

V

THE SECRET OF SUCCESS

THE SECRET OF SUCCESS IS INSIDE YOU. NOTHING CAN STOP YOU TO BE A SUCCESSFUL , EXCEPT YOU.

What is that one thing which lead us to success?

Who is there to help us for success ?

One thing, We must always keep in mind that whatever happens, such as a success or failure. We are the reason behind it. We must accept this bitter truth, instead of blaming someone.

I personally believe,

Hard work.

Dedication.

Will power.

Anger.

Patience.

Do we get a success with these words ?

No worries, I am not throwing something but I want you to understand these words deeply to have a success.

If not, no worries. Failure is always there so why not ? turning a failure into success.

What do you say ?

What do you think ?

Be cool and Be ready.

First thing, which always comes in our mind is that,

Am I ready for hard work ?

If yes,

Are you ready to work for 24 hours ?

If yes,

Success is coming to you.

It is like success is behind you.

It just, you need to understand about hard work. I am sure, an experience can be worst but the result of hard work will be very very sweet.

Second thing, which comes in mind is dedication.

Is there dedication inside you ?

If your loyalty is to get a success, then no one can stop you from being successful. Success will bow in front of you.

Third thing, which comes in our mind is will power.

Do I have that will power ?

Every person has some wishes but do I have the desire to get a success?

If yes,

Success is calling you.

Fourth thing, which comes in our mind is anger.

Do I become an angry when I do not finish my work.

Everyone feels angry but because of work, because of your promise of delivering the good and quality work..you get angry.

If yes,

You are going right.

Fifth thing, which comes in our mind is patience.

Do I have a patience inside me ?

Whatever work you do, If you do not have a patience..success will not come

If not today,

If not tomorrow,

But the day after tomorrow, success will definitely come.

Do you know ?

You have an abilities which can attract the magnet. If you understand this...,

It means, you are attracting success.

Always keep in mind that If he/she can do it then Why can't I?

It takes times, It takes much more time than expected. First, you need to invest that five keywords in you and see the result.

You will get better result and I am sure about it.

You can feel the success because the success is within you.

- **Success is within you.**

- **Celebrate the small things.**

- **If he/she can do then definitely you can.**

- **Be ready for struggle, if need a success.**

Quote No - 5

" Where were you ? What were you doing ? Where are you ? What are you doing ? It is not important but where you want to go that is very very important. - Nitesh More. "

VI

DESIRE

If I determined to do, then I have to do it. No matter, how much time it takes for it but for that, First become the king of that field and for this, your desire should be strong.

Success is within you and no one can stop it , but how strong is your desire to achieve that success.

I can do this.

I can do this anyhow.

My desire calls me all the time and says, go and get it.

It is your desire only, No one else.

Live with desire.

Sleep with desire.

Eat with desire.

Success will come to you because It is inside you,

What you do today, brings tomorrow.

If your desire burning like a fire, then nothing can stop you from getting a success. Neither any human being nor anything, nor any power. This will happen..when you have a strong desire. Your mind should be completely clear, no other thoughts, you should be crazy to get that desire.

As you go crazy to get your desire, people will get attracted towards you.

Everything is there to complete your desire.

Every person wants to be a successful in a shortcut way. No one wants to spend a time because they get scared inside.

Desire is a good thing but changing the desire again and again is not a good thing at all.'

If desire is strong then the path will find you and when the roads are found, it does not take time to reach your that desire.

The bad thing is that when we see a star, we start copying. So the problem is...after seeing someone, you are changing your desire then there is a serious problem.

Do not change your wishes again and again please.

All the great things that have happened in the history because of desire, and desire is one such a thing that gives us unlimited power to inspire us to reach that goal.

In the simple language,

A person has a desire and If he or she is crazy enough to get it then no one stop him/her to get a success.

- Do not kill your desire.

- Enjoy your desires.

- Be free and live with desires.

- Desires can take you towards your goal.

Quote No - 6

" It does not matter, How many times you fall but, After falling, You give up or get up that's only matters. - Nitesh More. "

VII
ATTITUDE

POSITIVE ATTITUDE CAN MAKE YOUR LIFE MORE BEAUTIFUL. IT CAN GIVE YOU EVERYTHING, WHAT ARE YOU LOOKING FOR. IT HELPS US FOR BETTER FUTURE.

Attitude is everything. Attitude is a very simple thing but It makes a big differences.

For example,

You have to take a photo but somewhere, you are thinking to change the angle. If you do this, you will get a different view of photo.

Whoever you are, your attitude tells that How the person you are.

You are the only one who knows, which path should go to follow the passion.

You are the only one who has his own strength and own ability.

What is your dream ?

What kind of attitude should be kept for it...? You know this better than anybody else and that attitude is inside you.

People should get inspired by your attitude, by your words, by your behaviour, by your work, by your thinking, by your mind.

If you have that sweetness in your talk, then people will come to you.

If you keep this type of attitude, people will not see whether you are a poor or rich. Your behaviour should be..., they have never seen such type of behaviour till date.

Sometimes our ego kills so many opportunities.

It is not necessary that people wish you first. You can also wish.

Today, who is a big or small. It just attitude you have...that's it.

When you made it,
People will be waiting to take your appointments.
They will be waiting to meet you.
They will be waiting to work with you.
They will be waiting to talk to you.
For this, your thinking should be positive in every situation.

You do not have to wait for perfection. You get the solution of any situation from your own thinking and it will come only because of your attitude.

Your mind should always be cool so that you always take a decision in peace and that is good for everybody.

If you find something wrong then you should fight to make it right.

Slowly, slowly, you will come to know about your improvement because of your attitude.

And of course,
Attitude is something that's make you a different person than others.
So do you want to be a different or
You want to be the same as others are.
The answer is in your hand which also decides your attitude.

- Keep this quality with you because attitude is everything.

- This attitude can give you everything.

- Any situation, always be positive.

- Be the change and see the change.

Quote No - 7

" I am falling in love with my brain because I am the driver of my brain. - Nitesh More. "

VIII

PURPOSE

LIFE HAS A PURPOSE OF SENDING YOU IN THIS BEAUTIFUL WORLD. HAVE YOU FOUND YOUR PURPOSE ?

What is your purpose?

Do you have any answer or are you just living a life without purpose?

If there is no purpose in life then I don't think, you are doing something better.

Without purpose, how can you improve yourself ?

If you want to achieve something in your life, then start searching for your purpose first.

If you don't know, what to do ? then what will you do ?

A purpose reminds you what to do and why I am doing this.

You must write down your purposes at least once in a day.

Today, peoples are running and If anyone ask? Where are you going ? someone is running that's why, I am also running.

I hope, you are not one of them.

Who is running without purpose.

This is happening because there is no purpose of your life with you.

Don't you feel ashamed of running like this ?

Are you used to it ?

Do you like to be like those?

Today, you too and your future generations will remain the same because If you do not have your own purpose, then what will happen to the future generation?

Can you imagine that ?

This is the right time to think about your purpose in life. Whatever till now happened, It is gone so please do not go in past.

You are at right time so think now and make a purposeful life.

You must ask to yourself,

What am I doing ?

Why am I doing ?

What is my purpose ?

Is this the right purpose of my life ?

How can I turn my dream into reality ?

How can I reach my goal by having a purpose in life ?

If you ask a small child, What is he doing ?

He will also say that I am playing a game for earning a points.

But we are not able to answer because we really don't know....?

What am I doing ?

And for why ?

And for what ?

And for whom ?

If you want something, do it now , do it, just do it and find your purpose.

Either you should follow your passion or whatever you are doing , make that work as a passion.

This world is yours, If you are living a purposeful life.

- Understand the purpose of your life.

- Live a purposeful life or leave it.

- Time to find your purpose, if not now then when ?

- You are the one who knows your purpose of your life, No one else.

Quote No - 8

" History can be created when you decide to create the history.

- Nitesh More. "

IX

AWESOME

AWESOME WORD BRING A SMILE . IT IS VERY EXCITING TO HEAR ABOUT AWESOME WORD.

ARE YOU HAVING THAT EXCITEMENT ?

ARE YOU HAVING AWESOME DAY ?

Last time, when you said that I am having an awesome day.

Do you remember ?

What was that awesome thing which bring a smile on your face..?

Everyone expects to have an awesome day but no one try to live in a present to have an awesome day.

An awesome day can bring a more fun in life. It can be more exciting but If you are available in present.

Actually, we have forgotten to celebrate the small things.

Actually, we have forgotten to appreciate others.

Actually, we have forgotten to enjoy the moment.

We feel that by following others can bring a happiness in my life.

Is it true ?

We feel shy to be in present.

May be,

Other things, which is happening in your mind right now.

First of all,

Stay away from mobile or use very less...if it is possible.

Do you have a plan for next day?

What do you do before sleeping ?

Never go to sleep without making a plan for next day. When you wake up in the morning, Read positive books, It will help you to have an awesome day.

Later, you can start your work.

Reading books is really helpful.

They are really best friends.

They always keeps you in profit.

They teach you better lesson.

If you really do this by heart, your day will be awesome.

When things goes as we planned, we feel good and we get happiness.

Below some sentence, which can help you to have an awesome day.

I am happy.

I am kind.

I am strong.

I am good at thinking.

I love myself.

I am enjoying a happy life.

I thank god.

I am beautiful.

I am enjoying laughing.

I love my work.

I love what I do.

Anyone can have an awesome day. It is in our mind. It is in our body. It is in our blood. It is inside you.

- What makes you feel awesome...

- Feel that awesomeness feelings.

- Make everyday awesome is in you.

- Be awesome.

Quote No - 9

" I believe, If you work to change your habits. You can change your tomorrow. - Nitesh More. "

X
ADVICE

GIVEN OR TAKEN BUT BE CAREFUL BECAUSE IT HAS A POWER TO MAKE YOU UP OR EVEN DOWN SO THINK BEFORE GIVING OR TAKING ANY ADVISE.

Is it necessary to take the advice ?

Getting advice from someone is really required.

Asking someone is different and asking yourself is totally different but still, we like to ask others because we have a confusion.

Is it ?

I am very concerned about advise.

We only take advise when we need it.

May be,

We take advice, if we do not trust ourselves and our own project.

It is very important to get an advice for better opinion but It is also very important to see that whom I am asking.

Normally, we ask advice from our family, from our friends, from our colleagues, from our relatives, from our neighbourhood, from our teachers, coaches and so on..

I am happy that you have chosen good peoples for taking an advice but before taking any advice from anyone...,

You must ask yourself...

Are those people at top of their respective fields?

Have they made any history?

Are they a good businessman ?

Can they be a good advisor?

Are they good as a counselor ?

Do they really care about you ?

Do you think those people will give you the right advise?

There are so many people who have not done anything but their mouth always speak.

The question is,

The person who does not know anything about your project.

Can he/she give a better advise ?

What advice will you take from those person who has not gone out of his town?

Can he be a good advisor?

The person who is not doing anything. How can he tell you ?

what is right or wrong ?

If you really want to get advise, then first you have to clear in your mind that no matter, what happens.., I have to do it. I am made for this purpose and I can do this.

I can do this is the sign of good confidence and I can only do is the sign of Over-Confidence.

If you want to get advice, Take it from someone who is specialize in that fields and If it is difficult to reach them, try to take an appointment.

Nowadays, It is very easy by Facebook, Twitter, Email, Insta. Use the social media to connect with them. It will take some time but you keep working.

That day is not so far.

The world is set on hope. No worries about.

If you can dream it, You can achieve it.

Let me tell you a story, just for a better understanding.

If you want to become a singer,

Will you ask to those people who does not have any idea about singing or you will ask to those, who are a top of singing fields.

May be, you can start meeting with singers, then meeting in studios, then meeting with music directors and then top of the music industry.

Advise taken from the expert of that field can make you better.

If a person knows nothing about that field, he can just demotivate you, nothing else.

Take advice carefully because it is your dream.

Nothing will happen to the adviser but it will definitely make you sad or happy.

\- Be careful about advise.

• 45 •

\- One advice can change your life or ruin your life.

\- Before taking any advice, see the background.

\- Do you really need an advice ?

Quote No - 10

" No one is here to understand you. Only you can understand to yourself because No one has a time to understand you. - Nitesh More. "

XI
VALUE

EVERYTHING HAS A VALUE BUT HUMAN CAME IN THIS WORLD WITHOUT VALUE BECAUSE THEY CAN EARN AS MUCH AS THEY THINK.

What is your value ?

Do you have any answer ?

The value of the value is never less or more..just our thinking decides the value of that value.

Our happiness also depends on our value. We start feeling pain, sad, disappointed, down.

When we know our value, our value does not hurt us but It keeps popping in our mind.

Every person has a 24 hours, even for the poor also and for rich too but how we use that 24 hours make a big difference. Some are just wasting those 24 hours. Some are just enjoying those 24 hours.

The person who is wasting, what will be his value ?

The person who is enjoying, what will be his value ?

By doing this, you do not understand the value of any person because everyone got only 24 hours then why in this society, few are rich and more of poor.

How do they use that 24 hours?

They just know one thing and that is their own value for next 24 hours. They know very well.

Let me explain by an example,

You have Rs.100

You gave that to other...still the same value.

After giving to other,

He tried to crush that Rs. 100 and even try to tear ...but still the same value.

After some time, he throw that note on a road and found someone else...still the value of that note is Rs. 100.

The reason behind is that, people will come in your life. They will try to put you down. They will try to break you. They will try to feel you embarrassed. They will do everything to make you feel bad.

If they do this also, they will not reduce your value because your value is decide by you, in your mind.

Who are you ?

What can you do ?

Your value was in past.

Your value is in present.

Your value will be in future.

Then why do you see yourself down, if something happens wrong with you for a sometime.

Nothing is last forever.

Why do we like the life of others.......?

Your value is in you.

You are the value of your life.

Enjoy your value respectfully.

- What is your value ?

- Who will cares about your value ?

- Understand your value or start working to make your value.

- Think, take action and create the value.

Quote No - 11

" Problem can be a problem or problem can be an opportunity.

- Nitesh More. "

XII

STAY

We can enjoy a life more by spending a time with family.

Most of the people like to spend a time with others and that is why, nowadays, everyone is away from family. Even if they at home also, they are busy with other stuff.

Things have changed very fast.

Family is the weak point for some peoples and other side, family is the strong point.

Living with family means to keep yourself in hell ?

Is that true ?

Whatever answer you have.

Just rethink about your family.

Stay with family because family can understand you better than anyone else.

Family can give you more happiness than anyone else.

This is the family that wants you to move forward.

This is the family that was with you in your bad time.

This is the family that helps you to understand right or wrong.

This is the family who understands your hidden pain.

This is the family who does not speak more but silently offers you something for your goodness.

Is this true or not ?

Everyone has a different experience but still I would like to say,
Please stay with family.
We like to spend more time with friends than family.
We like to spend more time with those people whom we do not know.
Family is always ready to support you but do you really care about them
?
Do you like by cheating by some people?
Do you still want to be with some people ?
What is right or wrong?
It does not mean anything to anyone.
People will come and go. There will be a family that will always be with you, so you have to decide whether to stay with them or leave them.
On this planet,
Family is a gift.
Do you know?
Time also leaves you.
Friends also leave you.
Relatives also leave you.
And so many other relations....but the family is something that always stays together.
As time passing, everything will be changed.
The rest will just keep on coming and going in life but what will always be together is your family.
Stay positive.
Stay humble.
Stay with family.

- Stay little more.

- Stay with someone, who understands.

- Stay today because no guarantee of tomorrow.

- Staying with someone is like caring.

Quote No - 12

" Be better or be the same. Choice is yours. - Nitesh More. "

XIII

BEST OF THE BEST

WHAT WAS THAT LAST MOMENT ?

WAS THAT BEST OF THE BEST ?

BEST OF THE BEST CAN BE ANYTHING BECAUSE ONCE THE MOMENT GONE, NEVER COME BACK THAT MOMENT SO MAKE EVERY MOMENT IS THE BEST OF THE BEST MOMENT OF YOUR LIFE.

Wherever you live, no matter how you live but your life should be the best of the best.

We are living a life by crying for small things and It had affected badly.

So the point is,

Do you really want to live a best of the best life ?

We want everything easily.

We want everything for free.

We are the laziest people on this planet.

We want everything in our hand.

If you want to become a better, then get up and start working.

Think about it.

Start doing a research.

Keep doing an experiment.

Put yourself in that more than 100%.

You can have the best of the best life, when you come out from the comfort zone.

Best of the best is a solution of your work.

Do the best.

Play the best.

Think the best.

Eat the best then everything will be the best of the best.

Do not consider any work as a work but do it as your passion.

How to be different from others?

By learning,

By reading,

By doing mistakes,

By doing hard work,

By keeping persistence.

Winners never give up, they just keep going.

Start living with the best of the best peoples to get the best, to give the best, to share the best ideas with them and taking their opinion. It will help you for your growth to be the best of the best.

Read the best books and try to make your thinking best of the best.

Everyone is the best but for me, I am the best of the best. I can and I am praying for being a best and I am ready to pay for being a best of the best version of mine because, This is my life and I want to be the best.

May be, it can be my ego.

May be, it can be my attitude but I wanna be the best...by doing, by working, by understanding, by earning in a right way to be the best of the best and this will lead to have a success in life.

Goals are for everyone but a person who spends all his time for his own goal. He will give his best of the best to achieve that goal.

Time will pass and you have to walk with the time.

Struggle makes you strong.

The failure will take you towards success.

Falling will force you to rise and walking will teach you to run.

To gain a success, It is natural to falling again and again but after falling, what do you do ? that is very important.

Just give yourself the best of the best towards work and see the changes.

Life will be much better than before.

- Which is your best of the best moment ?

- Enjoy your best of the best moments openly.

- **Understand the value of your best of the best moments.**

- **This moment will not come so enjoy every moment of your life.**

Quote No - 13

" Your thoughts can make you happy or sad in a next second so choose your thoughts carefully. - Nitesh More. "

XIV

TIME

TIME CAN BE GOOD OR BAD AND WE ARE RESPONSIBLE FOR OUR CURRENT SITUATION.

DO YOU ACCEPT THIS TRUTH?

IF YES, THEN CHANGE YOUR TIME BY CHANGING YOURSELF FOR BETTER LIFE.

Do not waste your time at all.

This is the only one thing in our life, in this world that will never come back so respect your time.

I would like to tell you about wasting of time.

It will help you to understand the time management very well.

You can earn money again...

You can make your house again...

No matter, how rich a person is or how poor person is but he can't bring a time back.

We as a human, always wait for a good situations. Sometimes, it can be right but it is always dangerous.

Every time is a good time. It just, you have to start . you have to take an action which actually, we don't do or may be fear we have.

The gone time will never come back.

Things will be started again but you can't start a gone time. Once it is gone means gone forever.

Our mind works differently. As per our thinking, our food, our activities and so on...,but time for everyone is same. Only 24 hours.

The day, when you start using your the 24 hours properly in your life. You will come to know the value of timing.

You will come to know that you are on right path of success.

I tell you a story,

Suppose, If you are getting a wages of Rs. 2400 for 24 Hours in a day.

Will you waste your time?

You can't because you are getting Rs.100 for every hour.

Now in the same way, time is also there.

Your hour is like Rs.100

If you lost that hour, You lost Rs.100

You can make the money again but the lost time will never earn.

After wasting every hour, you are destroying your life. May be, You can't see that but truly, It is happening and you are still unknown.

Sometimes, we used to say,

I will do it tomorrow,

But our tomorrow never come.

If there is an emergency, we manage immediately then why do we think in that way...?

Time is also an emergency.

Once gone,

Means gone forever.

- Use your time carefully.

- Value your time.

- Once gone, never come back so think before wasting.

- Invest in good things for better results.

Quote No - 14

" Nothing is changed and Nothing will be changed until you take a right or wrong decision. - Nitesh More. "

XV
MOTIVATION

Motivation is a type of machine which keep you motivated.

Is it possible?

Motivation is within us for a some time like when we read any motivational book, then you will find a motivation and after some time, back to normal life.

We get motivation, by watching motivational movies.

By listening motivational audios.

By reading motivational books.

By inspiring quotes.

By hearing inspiring stories and so on..

Can motivation will be with us forever ?

Let me tell you a story,

A woman said to a writer.

Your motivation book give me a motivation for a some time. I really don't like that.

A writer smiled and said,

From now, Do not eat anything and see a results.

A woman was angry on him.

Writer is just looking at her.

After some time, woman is going from there because she got an answer of writer's silence.

It is very simple but our mind does not accept this fact.

When you read a book, everything seems good. It gives hope in life but as soon as we stop reading, motivation goes.

What is the reason behind?

As we need a food to our body. Similarly, our brain needs a motivation on a daily basis to be motivated.

If it is not possible to read a book then listen motivational audios, watch motivational movies.

All the successful people in the world have a common habit that is to keep motivating themselves on daily basis.

They always keep a small diary of scheduling so that they manage a time to get a motivational stuff.

They believe,

Good thoughts can come anytime.

Better to write in a note and take an action.

Try to do this and you will feel the change.

Stay motivated and keep going.

- Motivation is must for everything.

- With this, you can achieve anything.

- Add daily motivation in your life.

- Feel the change of motivation.

Quote No - 15

" The difference between I am the best and I am only the best. I am the best is my confidence and I am only the best is my overconfidence.

- Nitesh More. "

XVI
ONCE AGAIN

FALLING IS GOOD BUT AFTER FALLING, WHAT DO YOU DO ?
ONCE AGAIN, DO YOU TRY ?
CAN YOU GIVE ONE MORE TRY ?

If you want to live a life once again then live a life today because no one can know that what will happen tomorrow ?

You can not enjoy your life tomorrow. Only you have a today to enjoy.

What will happen after 3 years?

What will happen after 5 years?

It is not in our hand but what we have is to make a plan and take an action to have a better future.

It is not written that whatever you planned, It will happen and then you will enjoy your life. Is it possible ?

It does not work like that so better why not enjoy today ?

It is very good to think about future but don't let the future dominate your present. The day, you do so...you are in the middle of the your past and future.

It clearly shows that you are ruining the present.

Every person knows that anything can happen at any time because today, there is no guarantee of anything.

When we buy electronics, at least, It has a guarantee of 1 year and in that 1 year...it gives a happiness to entire family.

Human life is worst than that.

Every person knows that next second, heart attack or accident or anything and you dead.

Everything is front of our eyes but still, we don't see.

Why are we not enjoying the present ?

We all are aware of this fact but still, we used to hurt others .

Stealing the money,

Killing someone,

Hurting someone,

And never ending list...,

You get happiness by doing this then keep on doing but the fact is, this happiness is for a some time and you must know this.

Life is beautiful but we have destroyed enjoying.

Enjoying the present is in our hand.

Past and future can not give you anything. Worries kills...again and again thinking about worries makes you weak and the truth is still unknown.

When a child born, everyone is so happy.

When he/she get married, everyone welcome them and gives a blessing and some gifts,

Some money and so on..

But when he/she dead, everyone is sad..even some of enemy also.

We are sad because we lost a loved one but when he/she was alive...

Is there anyone who understand them ?

Is there anyone who help them ?

Is there anyone who support them ?

Is there anyone who give a time to them ?

After death, we like to speak nicely about them but why not, when they are alive...?

Better to understand the value of person.

Respect him when he is alive.

Talk politely with them.

Spend time with them.

Appreciate them for small things.

If we do this, person feels that I have a some respect in this world.

Everyone has to die, but die in such a way that people remember you..

By your nature,

By your love,

By your politeness,

By making him comfortable,

By showing respect,

Because we have only one life and we should enjoy every moment of life.

- Try once again, this is not the end.

• 75 •

- Once again gives a hope of trying again.

- Feel and understand the value of once again.

- Your once again can change everything.

Quote No - 16

" My real friend is my mirror because It shows me, Who is my real competitor...? - Nitesh More. "

XVII
THOUGHTS

THOUGHTS HAS A SUPER POWER TO MAKE YOU HAPPY OR EVEN SAD IN THE NEXT SECOND.

CHOOSE YOUR THOUGHTS CAREFULLY.

Your thoughts are the reason behind your today's situation and will be the reason of your tomorrow's situation.

You better think about it.

It is said that the role of thoughts is important in our life because of those thoughts, ideas...people made a computers, made airplanes, made bulbs, and the never ending list.

If you are a positive person, you will spread a positivity and If you are a negative person then you will spread negativity, which is not good at all to you and for others.

Whatever your situation,

Wherever you go,

Your thoughts are always there. It just, which thoughts you love.

Human's potential is unlimited with thoughts and If your thoughts are awesome.

Most of the people think about negativity and because of that, their thoughts start working negatively.

I would like to tell you a story about how our mind works.

Once the principle went to a class and he told to the students.

Those students who are white, They are average in studies and those Students who are black, They are top in studies.

He only said because he just wanted to see..., what's happening ?

After 15 days,

Principle went to the same class and said that there was a slight error in the results. He apologised and said, white students did very well and black students are average.

He knew, What will happen ?

The truth is, principle has lied.

Why ?

For what ?

After 3 months,

When the result came. He found that white students are top in studies.

Principle came in the same class with a smile and shared entire story with papers.

He said that,

What we learn from this story...., nothing happens. If you are a white or black. Everything happened because of our thinking.

When I said average, your thinking started about average thinking and mind also started working like that.

When I said top, your thinking started about top thinking and mind also started working like that.

All those successful people have a clear picture in their mind about future and because of that, their plans, actions,thoughts and of course, always being positive to keep them motivated.

- Think big.

- Add daily new thoughts in your life.

- Thoughts can make you happy or even sad.

- Be positive and enjoy your life.

Quote No - 17

" Change is good but for what reason, We are changing that is the only change is good. - Nitesh More. "

XVIII
BELIEVE

OUR BELIEVE GIVES A STRENGTH TO OUR IDEA. IT GIVES A CONFIDENCE. IT HELPS FOR BETTER PLANNING.

If you don't believe yourself then why would the world believe in you.

You are going to meet so many peoples in this beautiful world.

Your family,

Your relatives,

Your neighbors,

Your friends,

Your colleagues and so many other more people.

Those who will try to demotivate you by saying such as,

You can not do this.

Look at yourself,

Don't do it.

It's not in your hand.

Look at your family, if they could not do anything . how can you do ?

Just stop thinking about that but you do not need to stop because this is the only situation in your life where they are trying to break your dream. They are trying to keep you away from your dream.

You are the only person who is responsible for this. Only you..no one else because if you do not believe in you then why would the world do it ?

If you have even a small idea and you believe in that idea,

I guarantee, you can do it.

Once you have shown confidence in yourself, you do not need anyone else faith. Just you need your faith.

Whenever you go to others to speak about the idea, just for opinion.

You are probably afraid of idea. Will that work or not ?

It means, you are not confident about that idea. There is something wrong in somewhere.

People can share their opinion but inside, They will be thinking... If the person who is not confident about his idea. How can this work ?

They will not say to you because It can be uncomfortable to them.

You are the hero of your idea and you are the king of that idea. No one can do it better than you because that idea is just made for you only.

Most important thing in life is to just believe in yourself. If you do this, You can achieve anything, you want to achieve.

The saddest part is that,

These type of things are not teaching in our school.

We are hoping that One day, these types of things will be started.

The time will come where no one will believe in you but no need to worry.

You must always keep in mind that I believe in me.

I can do this.

God made me for this.

I am strong.

I can make my dreams come true.

Live life as you want and for this, you have to believe in yourself because you are a creator of your life.

Just be as you are.

Most of the time, we live with narrow minded people and because of that, our thinking is also becoming narrow minded. Always keep a distance from narrow minded peoples.., if you want to do something in your life.

We wait for the perfection. We think that when the situation is good then I will do but the bitter truth is, situation will never be perfect.

We always wait for the good situation and that is the our problem and the saddest thing is, we are expert to give the reasons.

If you want something, Trust yourself and get it.

Look at the dream.

Believe that dream.

Try to achieve it.

You will fall.

You will afraid.

You will be frustrated.

You will feel depressed but you do not have to stop, you just have to walk because you are the one who believes in your dreams.

Why are you waiting ?

Why to quit ?

Loser says, No

You are not a loser.

May be, you can fall 1000 times but the winner is always rise for fighting and you are a fighter.

It is very easy to defeat but it is very difficult to stand in the field.

You keep on hoping that you are going to reach your goal and this will happen...when you start believing in you. When you start believing on your dream.

If you believe in yourself, nothing can stop you to reach your goal.

- Always believe in yourself.

- Believe gives more confidence.

- Believe it the key to success.

- Just believe and do it.

Quote No - 18

" If you don't have time to think about yourself, Then who will think ?

- Nitesh More. "

XIX

GOAL

Goal help us to achieve our dream. Without goal, Life is zero.

Goal is a goal. Not the gold aah...Nowadays, Gold rate is touching the sky.
Let's go to our goal.
What is goal ?
G-Great
O-Opportunity
A-At
L-Life
This is called goal.
Do we really think about our goal or just keep saying ?
I believe, If there is no goal, there is no life.

This is also true because If you do not have a goal, then your life was the same yesterday, even today and always be like this. You are just living a life without goal.

You know what, everyone has their own goal. I am sure, You will be having one of the best goal to have a bright future. You are the only one , who can know your goal, Not anyone else.

Your goal that can make you stand out from others to help you to do better than others.

If you think little more calmly, then you will know.

If still....,no problem at all. I am giving an example to know better about goal. Now you just think that you have to go to meet a special person. (to meet a special person is your goal.) just assume, but it is far away.

What will you do now to meet them ?

First, you will research that If I have to go there to meet that special person then I will find the information about that place. Right.

After getting the information, you will be ready and come out of the house. Right.

Then after that, You will sit in a van or start a van if Own...Right.

You are happily inside. Sweet smile is coming outside because you are going to meet a special person. You are so happy but at one point, you see there are so many roads. You are thinking, which path to take. It will be restless to you but If you have a goal then you will catch the same path that leads to your goal which means, the path leading to meet a special person.

This similar goes for a goal.

You have to go to step by step and If you don't know your goal then what is the difference ? you can go by any road.

Still you did not understand..?

Once a man was waiting at the bus stop,

The other person came and asked?

Where will this bus go ?

The first one looked at him and said, where do you want to go ?

The other one said, I do not know.

Hearing this, the first man said to him. Catch any, what does it matter?

Similar like, if you have a goal then you will reach by taking a step by step but if you don't have any goal then take any step.

It does not matter.

- To set a goal, follow the daily schedule.

- Don't shy to ask anything related to your goal.

- To celebrate small things because those small moment will not come back.

- To ask anything, if it related to your goal.

Quote No - 19

" Tomorrow will come with new opportunities but not for you, For other's.

- Nitesh More. "

XX
DEPRESSION

Depression is such a disease that we are embrace to tell our family, doctors, friends because we feel, If I say... they will make a fun of me in the society.

If you are going through depression and you won't see any way.

Stay away from depression as soon as possible.

May be, your time is going but this is not your end because you are better than this and you can do better than before.

I can understand that, this is very difficult time right now but still, I would say that every problem has a solution.

You are having a bad chapter in your life and not a bad life in one chapter.

We ourselves call negativity to ourselves and the same negativity helps to put you into depression.

There are so many peoples in the world who are in depression.

Are they really want to get out of it ?

We are here in this beautiful world to have a positive life and I am sure, you can also have it. If they can have then definitely, you can also have.

You have that attitude to face the depression and fight with it. Your life is in your hands and you can make it more beautiful. No one can put you in a depression until you give yourself a permission to put yourself in a depression.

Your people are waiting for you because you are a world for them.

Your family,
Your relatives.
Your friends,
Are waiting to meet you because they can't see you in depression.
They just want to see you happily.
They just want to feel the changes in you.
You are very beautiful and world needs you.
Why are you in past moments ?
Why are you hurting yourself by remembering past moments ?
Hey, look ahead...

You will see happiness when you remember good moments and when you see bad moments, you feel bad. Whatever happened is happened. It has gone and there is no meaning to remember that. By doing that...you are just hurting to yourself.

Do you know that ?
Do you want to be like that ?
Do you have time to be like that ?
Do you want to stay in a room alone ?
Don't you like to spend a time with others ?
How can you do this ?

This is the right time to have a change. Please feel the change and change yourself and come out with a new version of you.

Let's enjoy my friend.

- Be free to feel better.

- Be the change of your life.

- Time to heal yourself and you can heal.

- Don't take life too seriously.

Quote No - 20

" Laziness will not change you. You change to laziness. - Nitesh More. "

XXI

STOP BUTTON

WHERE IS YOUR START BUTTON?

WHY ARE YOU USING STOP BUTTON?

YOUR START BUTTON IS WITHIN YOU BUT YOU ARE SEARCHING IN OTHERS.

What has stopped you?

Why are you not starting ?

Whom to wait for...?

Are you waiting for someone's permission?

Friends,

Wherever you are...,

In any situation...

You can start your life again.

You can start your new journey.

Today,

More than half of the world's population is struggling with the disease of depression because they like depression and that is why, you have taken a stop button in your mind.

The real reason for that disease is you only. Don't blame to anyone. You must accept this. You are the one who called this disease.

You can heal your life and start a new life because this is your life and you have the rights to live fully. You may not even know, what is happening ? but day by day, you are going down. You are becoming weak. You know that but still, you don't understand.

Today is the day who helps to bring a tomorrow, so live today and leave that stop button and start use button.

You are afraid,

You are worried about what people will say…, If I tell them about current situation.

No one cares and that's the fact so forget others and think about yourself.

First you need to change to feel a better to have a changes in you and in the society.

Today, Everything is possible.

You are still there because you have kept a stop button with you and because of that, you are not starting a new things to discover about yourself.

One stop button has destroyed your life and one start button can make your life more beautiful.

Everything happens in our life for a reason and that reason can be good or bad.

Why we stop living a life?

We stop living a life for a small things, If anything goes wrong…that's not the end.

Life is to live and not to leave.

You must learn to forgive people and move on in life. Don't be sit at a one place. Start a new journey and see the changes.

The more you think, then more you will go down. So keep that start button in your hand .

Open your new book of your life and enjoy the new version of yourself.

- This is the right time for start button.

- No one has stopped you.

- You do things for yourself so at least, think about it.

- **Be ready for a new life.**

Quote No - 21

" You can stop but your thinking is unstoppable. - Nitesh More. "

Author of Two Life changing books called " Feel the change" and " Jivan Jivan Aahe ka ? "

Currently, He is working as an Assistant Director and a Script Writer in the Indian Film and Television Industry.

He has written, Directed and Produced a Hindi Short Film Called " BASURI-The flute" and a script writer of Marathi Short film Called " NAKKI CHUK KONACHI ? "

He has directed a Marathi Ahirani Song Called " MANA DILVAR KAYA RE VAAR "

Studied from Night college, Mumbai.

He loves watching a movies, Writing, reading a books, Playing a cricket and travelling.

" MY MARATHI BOOK "

Enter Caption